# Pocket Prayers
# for Teachers

*Other books in the series:*

*Pocket Celtic Prayers*
compiled by Martin Wallace

*Pocket Graces*
compiled by Pam Robertson

*Pocket Prayers*
compiled by Christopher Herbert

*Pocket Prayers for Children*
compiled by Christopher Herbert

*Words of Comfort*
compiled by Christopher Herbert

# Pocket Prayers
# for Teachers

Reflections and prayers
in challenging times

David W. Lankshear

Illustrations by Craig Cameron

The National Society
*Leading Education
with a Christian Purpose*
Church House Publishing

National Society/Church House Publishing
Church House
Great Smith Street
London SW1P 3NZ

Published 2002 by National Society Enterprises Ltd
ISBN 0 7151 4983 0
Copyright © David W. Lankshear 2002
Illustrations © Craig Cameron 2002

Tel: 020 7898 1557;
Fax: 020 7898 1449;
Email: copyright@c-of-e.org.uk

Cover design by Church House Publishing
Printed in England by University Printing Press, Cambridge

# Contents

This book is dedicated
to Laura Williamson
and all other teachers
doing a 'proper' job

# Foreword

These prayers are different.

Different because they are written for teachers by a teacher; different because they actually do put into practice the advice in the old hymn 'to take it to the Lord in prayer'; different because they are a meditation, a conversation, an expression of trust, as well as a prayer – as, at least, I usually think of it.

If anyone really wants to know how teachers think, or to understand what lies at the heart of being a teacher, then these prayers tell the story. Every parent should read this book. And every newly appointed government minister for schools should read it as a set book, to see that the issues that occupy the minds of teachers at the end of the day are not the need for new policies and new initiatives. Their interests and concerns, their aspirations and hopes, are with the children and young people, whom they have chosen, through their profession, to serve.

In commending this book to teachers as a down-to-earth, meaningful approach to prayer, I realize that I should be taking on board that this approach to prayer is as relevant to me as to the teacher.

Right away, it brings the day's cares and hopes into a new perspective. I can see the clouds giving place to a little sunlight.

Ron Dearing

*In his many roles in education, Lord Dearing has produced reports on the National Curriculum and the future of Higher Education. His most recent task was to chair the Church Schools Review Group for the Church of England.*

# Introducing the prayers

In the pages that follow you will find a variety of reflections on topics drawn from school life. They are written in a style that regards prayer as a discussion with a beloved father.

The word 'Abba', which is usually translated as 'father' in the English versions of the Bible, is used by children in Israel as a name for their fathers; perhaps it corresponds to our words 'daddy' or 'dad'.

These prayers are therefore written as one side of a conversation with a beloved and wise 'dad', whom I address as 'Lord' because that is what comes naturally to me. These reflections to some extent pray my own experience of children and of schools. I offer them in the hope that they will enable other teachers to pray their own experience.

The reflections are in four groups. The first group and the longest is about individual children, for it is individual children that we seek to educate, not classes or tutor groups. All the names are invented, although many of the characters are not. Some of the characters may strike chords with your experience; feel free to change the names to make the prayers more personal to you.

The second group is about issues that affect all children, although their impact on individuals may be different. They deal with some of the difficult areas for teachers and others who work with children and young people.

The third group reflects the school year and some of the events that may occur in it. The life of the school as an institution is reflected in some of these prayers.

The final group is about teachers themselves. The order of these groups and the balance of material in them is deliberate and reflects the priority that most teachers give to the children in their care above their own needs.

If they are relevant, you may choose to pray these prayers yourself. It is more likely that they will strike chords for you that will stimulate you to talk with God about your own children, your colleagues, your school and the joys and challenges of being a teacher.

At the end of the book are some thoughts about ways in which some teachers have taken a more structured approach to their prayer life.

# Prayers about
# individual children

# For a good child

Lord, I want to pray for Adam today. He is so quiet – no trouble. What is he thinking? He gets on with the work – does it well – but is it as good as he could do? Does he ever get excited? Does he ever get so absorbed that he forgets to behave well or fails to do what he is told?

Is he ever naughty, Lord? It is strange, but I sometimes think it would be a good thing if he were.

What am I saying? Am I really suggesting that it would be better if a good child was sometimes naughty?

Well, perhaps, what I would like to be sure of is that he is relaxed and happy enough to be naughty; that the goodness is not just a fear of being bad.

There are more pressing worries in my class, and you know all about those. But, while we are talking about Adam, it would be reassuring if – just once – he would knock over a water pot, say a rude word into a silence, or even be cross. Once would be enough, but once would be reassuring.

# For an overactive child

Where do I start about Bronwen? She is like a rubber ball: always bouncing around, usually in the wrong place. Her work – when she does any – is a mess, and all her brain seems to be used in finding new ways to be cheeky or to disrupt others. She can't sit still for an instant; even other children in the class are beginning to get tired of the chaos she causes.

What do I do about Bronwen, Lord?

Yes, I know that she is made in your image and that I am meant to honour your image in her and to love her as your Son loved us; but . . . on a wet Friday towards the end of the autumn term that is hard – I mean hard to almost impossible.

And my colleagues are not much help, with their 'I know that she is difficult, but if you could just stop her . . . '

As if you could *just stop* Bronwen doing anything when you have not got her pinned down.

I don't know what to do about Bronwen, Lord – not on my own. I need your help to reach that fizzing mind and all that misused energy and find ways for her to channel them into something positive.

I know that with you nothing is impossible; so I would really appreciate some help with Bronwen, please.

# For a gifted child

I caught her at it the other day, Lord; I am talking about Chloe. It was that deep sigh and the raised eyebrows when I said something that she thought was wrong. This was followed by the question, so very polite, that showed me that I had made a mistake about the evolution of dinosaurs – again!

I know that she is probably more intelligent than I am and that her parents have both got PhDs, but just at the moment I am the teacher and she is the pupil.

Give her patience, Lord, to cope with the short-comings of her teacher.

Give me patience, wisdom and humility, Lord: patience to cope with the frustrations of teaching her in a class where she is the brightest; wisdom to accept that, although she has greater potential than I have, there is still much that I can give her; humility to take joy in her success and her insights, even when the speed of them bewilders me.

But above all this, Lord, let her – with all her gifts and potential – have a normal, happy childhood, before she assumes the burdens and responsibilities that her gifts will bring.

# For a child with special needs

Lord, today I want to talk to you about Daleep.
He is so brave in the way that he deals with school.
For him it is a constant challenge just to arrive in
school on time, let alone cope with the playground,
the corridors and the classroom. Yet he is cheerful
about it.

Such stubborn, cheerful courage deserves the best
from his friends and from me, so I ask for your
blessing on Daleep.

I also ask for your help to teach him well and
according to his needs so that his courage is
matched by our response.

The wheelchair has stopped being a problem,
really; we are all used to it and he gets around so
well. The problem is to remember his hearing and
the need to be alert to whether he can see my face.

You know his potential, Lord: all that he might
achieve. Somehow, we have to provide him with
the education that will help him achieve it, not a
cocoon that – with the best of intentions – will
get in the way.

It should not be difficult, Lord, but sometimes it is hard to balance his needs with those of others in the class.

Lord, this day and every day, I ask your blessing on Daleep.

# For children experiencing difficulties at home

Lord, there are children in my class whose parents
are in difficulties; relationships under strain. Today
I am thinking particularly about Ella, but she is not
the only one. She is tense, her work is suffering,
and her fun with her friends is muted. She is often
missing from school for the smallest reasons. There
is nothing I can do for her parents – they are in your
hands – but how do I help Ella, Lord? How do I help
the others like her?

How do I sustain them through the difficulties;
the break-ups that may come; the worry; the fear?

Just keeping things stable is a challenge. Helping
Ella get through the day without adding to her
worries seems to be a triumph.

I offer Ella and the others into your care and
keeping. Help me to support them; and to give them
the stability that they need, as soon as possible.

# For a child with an emerging talent

Lord, this has been a really good day. Well, most
of it was about average for a wet Friday; and then
I read this story written by Fatima. When I had read
through it once I went back and read it again. It
was wonderful, the way she used some of the words.
I mean, not all of them, but there were two or three
sentences that were fresh, new, and original.

They weren't her parents' words: this was class work.
They weren't her neighbours' words: I have read their
stories and they are different. These were her own
words, put together to express her own thoughts.

It is just possible that there is real talent here,
just beginning to show out of the bud. In my class –
my responsibility to nurture. What a challenge!

Thank you, Lord, for her talent and for the chance
that you have given me to develop it with her.

# For an unpopular child

There are some of your children, Lord, who
never seem to get along with their classmates.
Whatever they do they are on the outside of the
group. It must be very hard to want to be liked
and yet to be unpopular; excluded; left out.

Why does this happen to them?

Are you giving them strength for the task that you
have for them later? Are they the next generation
of your prophets?

Or is it much simpler: is it something that they do
or say? Will it change next week, or next month?

This is not a happy position for a child. Georgia
needs help and support.

How do I help and support her, Lord?

How can I help Georgia and others like her
without marking them out and making them
even more unpopular?

# For a caring child

Whenever someone is hurt, Harry is there. Whenever someone needs help, Harry is there. He is not very good at his class work – he is not clever – but, Lord, what a gift you have given him!

The gift of caring, of being there for others, of being able to see their need and respond to it.

It is a gift, Lord, but also a burden.

Who cares for the carers, Lord? Who supports those whose whole talent seems to be in supporting others?

We must educate – we are a school – but what about Harry? How do we educate him? What does he need? How can we respond? How can we show that we value his gifts?

He is a lovely, caring person. Lord, in all that we do, may he retain those precious gifts.

# For a 'natural leader'

They have done it again, that little group over there.

I have made a suggestion, Lord, trying to leave things open, and they all glance at Isabel. If she nods, they all say 'Yes'. If she shakes her head, they all say 'No'.

It's as if the only one with the ability to make a decision is Isabel. Well, that is not quite true, now I think about it. Isabel is just a natural leader. Whenever a group forms and she is part of it, she ends up leading it. A special gift from you, Lord?

But if it is a gift, what a responsibility! Yes, I know: part of being a leader is being able to cope with the responsibility; but even so . . .

How do we educate such a character, Lord? How do we develop that gift, when so often the existence of the gift is a source of conflict? If she is the 'natural leader' and I am the teacher, inevitably we are going to clash over who decides what the class will do – which brings me back to my starting point: those quick looks to check that what I have suggested is approved.

Another thought occurs to me: sooner or later leaders are rejected, or their place is taken by another more charismatic than they are. How do we prepare them for rejection; give them the strength to live with it, to shrug it off?

It seems so good to be the one who is looked up to, but as I think about it, life is complicated for them too; so today, Lord, I offer Isabel to your care.

# For a child in trouble

She stands there, outside the Headteacher's room, looking miserable and frightened, but trying so hard to be brave and defiant.

I don't even know what she has done this time. I can only guess. From the look of it, a fight was involved; but probably the major sin was not the fighting but what led up to it.

Lord, do you get tired of this, your child, and the turmoil of her life? We do! She is always in trouble; always breaking the rules; almost always sullen and defiant. She doesn't seem to enjoy her life much, but must she make others miserable too?

Now I think about it, there were times when the people of Israel were like that. Hosea taught us about your forgiving love. Your Son showed us his love in perfect action.

So you see, I know the theory, Lord; but your Son was perfect and we are not – so we really struggle with Jade.

Now she has gone, called into the Head's room. As she meets her fate for today, Lord, I offer Jade to you. Help her and care for her, Lord, and help us as we try to help her and care for her in your name – and all the others, too.

Through the door I have just heard: 'You are the worst-behaved girl in the school!' I wasn't listening; the Head was using her 'playground' voice. It is true, Lord: Jade is the worst-behaved girl in the school. It is good to face the truth about yourself; but, merciful Father, let her also know hope and love.

# For a loner

As I glanced around the playground this lunchtime,
Lord, I could see him quite clearly among the
milling, swirling groups of children.

Standing on the edge in a little cocoon of silence,
alone; apparently quite happy. He doesn't look at
the others much. There is no obvious longing to join
their games. He is absorbed in his own thoughts.

What are they, Lord? Where does he go when he
is not with us? Is he happy to be on his own? Or
is this learned behaviour, or a defence against the
possibility of rejection?

I am sure you know; but we do not seem to come
to a mind.

Some of my colleagues think he is disturbed,
withdrawn and unhealthy; they try to force him
into social situations. Others seem grateful that
there is a quiet child who is no trouble; they are
content to let him be.

Who is right?

Most of the time, we don't discuss him – there are
more pressing issues – but just for once, Lord, my
thoughts have turned to Kevin. Will he grow out

of this? Is he a great prophet or artist in the making? Or will he be a wanderer, a tramp, or a hermit?

What is your plan for Kevin, and how should we best help it forward?

# For a child from a 'home of faith'

Lord, you know me: I fuss a lot; I worry about things that others ignore; but – you made me that way, so here I go again.

It is about Liam, Lord. He comes from such a good home, where people who take their religion seriously surround him. They go to church regularly; say their prayers; and live lives full of faith in you.

Now I am not complaining about that; these are good people, Lord, seriously good people.

It is just – well, where is free will in this? Where is there space for Liam to rebel a little: to make up his own mind and come to his own decision?

Does he need spiritual room, Lord, and is it our job to provide it?

His parents have responded to your call, Lord – have made you the centre of their lives – but will Liam hear your call to him, above the singing and praying that surrounds him?

Am I fussing and worrying too much? Perhaps so; but what happens to Liam when the crisis of faith comes? If the crisis comes?

He is your child, Lord; help us meet his needs.

# For a 'chatterbox'

This is about Mollie, Lord. Does she ever stop talking? Words bubble from her all day. When others struggle to articulate a thought, with Mollie it feels as if thoughts only exist if they are articulated. For her, life seems a joyous exciting place that must be discussed instantly to be made real.

This can be exciting, stimulating and great fun, Lord, at the right time and in the right place. Last week she started to chatter in the middle of the SATS. The week before, the visitor leading school worship was so stimulating in the first part of his talk that it had to be discussed immediately, and none of my class heard the rest of what he had to say because Mollie was talking so much.

Trying to stop her, Lord, is like trying to turn off her personality, or to turn back the tide with a bucket and spade. On the other hand, there are twenty-nine others in the class, and they should have a chance to talk; they might have something really interesting to say. And while we are about it, Lord, I would like to get a word in edgeways, occasionally.

There is also silence, Lord: what a blessed thing silence is. But if Mollie was in the room and there was silence, we would only be worrying that she was ill!

I am not really complaining, Lord; we appreciate
the bubble and flow of ideas. But peace and quiet
is wonderful.

# For a 'distressed' child

I am told that Nathan is disturbed, Lord. He can certainly be rather odd at times, but so can some of the others in my class, so nothing unusual there.

It seems that he has a problem with relationships; that he has not learned how to relate well to his peers and to adults. That appears to be true, but how does saying it help, Lord? When he loses control and lashes out because he is frustrated, and leaves two others in the class in tears and work ruined, does it help to know that he has a problem forming relationships?

What I want to know is: how do I help him and – perhaps more importantly for everyone else – how do I help prevent his outbursts? Given that we can't change his mother or improve their housing, what can we do that will make a difference?

I know that he has a problem, Lord. I guess if I were living in two cramped rooms with an alcoholic mother I would probably be worse than he is, but that is not the point.

How can we offer hope; give him a chance to grow into a mature adult? How can we keep everybody else – their work, their worries – cared for while we deal with him?

Lord, I believe that you are in control of this situation; I just wish that somehow you would take me into your confidence.

I don't know what to do about Nathan, Lord, so I offer him to your care and mercy. Help, Lord!

# For a 'disaffected' pupil

He's given up, hasn't he, Lord? Oliver, I mean – just given up? It was always a struggle, finding a reason for him to keep trying, but just lately he seems to have lost the little drive that he had.

I don't think any of the males in his family have worked for years, so telling him that if he works hard at school he will get a good job is like trying to persuade an English batsman to play a long innings.

You and I know he *could* learn. You know what would make him want to learn, but I wish that I did.

I tried, Lord, I really tried, but you can't make someone learn when they don't want to; when they don't see the point. So . . .

Am I giving up too? Not good enough, is it, Lord? If I admit defeat, then I am giving up on him, just as he is giving up on himself.

So all right, I won't give up, but, help, Lord, what do I try next? Just a hint would help.

Lord, I am listening . . .

# For a child from
# a 'home without faith'

Paul does not come to religious education, Lord.
His parents have exercised their right to withdraw
him from what they describe as a 'waste of time'
and a 'ridiculous concern with a non-existent deity'.
How does that make you feel, Lord? It worries me.

It is the parents' right, but what about the child?
Should Paul have the opportunity to learn that there
are people who do not share his parents' secular,
materialistic views?

What could he lose?

If faith were foolish – rubbish – at least he would
understand what the rubbish is about. Perhaps his
parents fear that it is not rubbish.

I don't understand it, Lord; if I did, I guess I wouldn't
be talking to you like this.

So the parents have decided; and we are powerless,
and Paul will learn nothing of Jesus or Muhammad
but what he hears in the playground and the street.

O Lord, I place Paul into your care.

I think that he really needs it.

# For a happy child

Thank you for Qasim, Lord. He cheers me up so often. It seems that you have given him such a cheerful disposition that it rubs off on those around him and even sometimes on me.

What a gift that is. He is not the brightest, nor the most athletic child in the room, but he never seems to place too much emphasis on things like that. He enjoys doing a variety of different things during the day and doing most of them reasonably well. Not too many disasters; not too many triumphs; but quite a deal of fun on the way.

My colleagues think that I am potentially something of a depressive. They accuse me of looking for difficulties and problems even when they do not exist. So I refuse to worry about how he copes with major disasters; perhaps they won't happen to him. I am certainly not going to create one in order to equip him to cope with others later in life. I will just enjoy having him in the class, and thank you for his effect on the rest and on myself.

Thank you for Qasim, Lord.

# About Sports Day

Well, here it is again: Sports Day. The annual collection of triumphs, tears, hard-luck stories and arguments about the parents' race.

And the sun is shining, so there is no excuse! Thank you, Lord!

And there is Robert, with that twisted foot. How are we going to give him a chance of a good day? Asking him to hold one end of the finishing tape while everyone else runs past is not going to work this year; I just know it. What about Robert, Lord?

And then there is Sara. This is her one day of triumph in the year, Lord. You did not give her many brains, but she runs so beautifully! May this day give her the joy and strength that she needs to carry her through the rest of the year of struggle with letters, numbers and school rules.

So it is Sports Day. On this most mixed of days, may there be a good spread of smiles and may the worst problem be sunburn.

# For a neglected child

Have you seen the way he looks this morning, Lord? Tom, I mean; look at him! How could any parent send a child to school looking like that?

I know that he doesn't have school uniform – or at least, if he has, he never wears it – but does he have to come in looking like that? There is a hole in the knee of his trousers; he smells and looks as if neither he nor his clothes have been washed in the last week. His hair is a tangled mess. It makes me mad to see him like this, Lord; I mean, what chance has he got?

I know, I know. Calm down! React professionally!

Pull him in from the playground with the excuse that Mrs Smith, the welfare assistant, needs his help with a job before school starts; then she will clean him up a bit and tidy him up, and it should not be too bad for him in class today.

But, Lord, we do this so often; are we protecting him, or spoon-feeding and protecting his careless parents?

Does nobody love him?

Silly question, I know. You do.

And so do his parents, even if they can't look after him as we would wish.

Sustain us, Lord, as we attempt to sustain Tom.

# A prayer of triumph

She's got it, Lord, at last. I never thought that Uzma would ever master the decimal point, but there it is! She's got it!

Thank you, Lord, on her behalf as well as mine. Thank you.

I know that she may forget it tomorrow, and that come the SATS it will definitely have gone. Never mind; today she has got it, and for that I am truly grateful.

Uzma is such a pleasant child to teach – she is so ready to try – and yet anything to do with numbers just seems to convert her brain to jelly.

What happens in her head, Lord? Is there something missing there – a bump of numeracy omitted? Or did we fail to spot that she missed a vital link somewhere early on in her mathematical education?

Should I go back over old ground with her to find that missing link, or do I just accept what happened today and build on that? For today, Lord, she got it!

May it happen again tomorrow.

# For a quiet child

I wrote the reports, Lord, and then looked back at those that had been written last year, just to check for potential problems. It was fine until I read Vicky's. For three years in a row, her reports have said that she should try to make more contributions to class discussion, or that she is too quiet – which comes to the same thing.

Have we stopped to ask why she is quiet?

Is she thinking it all out?

Is she asleep?

Do others shout her down too easily?

Is she politely waiting her turn to be asked?

The phrasing of the reports implies that the fault is with her. Why do we blame her for being quiet?

Perhaps we are at fault for not making the space for her to speak, or perhaps you have just given her a quiet nature. If either of these is the case, then she is not to be blamed.

So what do I do, Lord?

Should I begin by writing that report again and this time finding something constructive to say? I thought that you might think that.

# For an attention-seeking child

'That child, William, is at it again,' they said. 'Such dreadful behaviour; attention seeking, that's all it is. We must ignore him. It only causes trouble if you reward attention seeking.'

It is strange, Lord, this reaction from my colleagues. They are good people. I don't know why they react like this to William's behaviour. Do they never stop to ask why a child should behave badly in order to attract attention? Could it be that he is not getting the level of attention that he needs?

Perhaps in rationing out the time and attention that we think we have to give, William's share does not meet his needs at this point in his life.

Do we help him by giving him less attention, Lord?

Who will suffer if we give him more?

While we do not even discuss these questions William continues to behave badly to get our attention, and to punish him for his bad behaviour we give him only just enough attention.

This has to stop, doesn't it, Lord?

Help us, Lord, to attend to William even when he does not scream for attention.

# For a child with a new sibling

Xavier came in this morning looking very cheerful.

'My mum has just had a baby,' he said.

This baby is his first sibling; he has been the only child for quite a long time, Lord. Now I think about it, this new baby has a different father from Xavier.

'Is it a boy or a girl?' I asked.

'It's a girl,' he said. 'They are going to call her Yvonne.'

So, Lord, this is a prayer for the family: for Xavier, and the adjustments to the relationships within his family that he will have to make; for Yvonne, to welcome a new child into the world; and for the new Mum and Dad, and all the challenges that they face.

It is good news, really: a new life, new experience for Xavier and, I hope, stability within the family. Be with them, Lord, as they work through the changes and live with the joy.

Oh, and remind me, Lord, to listen out for the comments of the other children in the class and to take action if there is any teasing. Why there should be I don't know, but that has not stopped there being teasing in the past.

# For a clumsy child

She has done it again! The paint pots are all over the floor, and the cleaners will be complaining to the Head about the mess within five minutes of coming into this room.

How am I supposed to stop Zara making a mess? She is just so clumsy, Lord: always slightly off balance; arms always slightly out of control.

It is not her fault. I have read the records; there is something in them about a problem when she was born.

She may have to live with her clumsiness for the rest of her life if she does not learn to compensate for it.

We will have to live with the results for the rest of her school days.

I will have to live with the cleaners' complaints, this evening and every evening for the rest of the year.

Give me patience, Lord. Help me to stay calm and support her, so, at least, things get no worse.

Give her patience, Lord, to cope with her problems and with insensitive adult responses to them.

# Prayers about growing up

# About puberty

Sometimes as I look round at this lot, Lord, I wonder what will become of them. Here they are, quietly working, for once! Interested in what I have asked them to do – an ordinary class, some bright, some willing, some charming, some brittle. One day soon, puberty will kick in; hormones will fly uncontrolled; and a whole new world of challenges, hazards, joys and mistakes will open up for them.

When you invented people, Lord, why did you include puberty?

Isn't there a better way of getting from childhood to adulthood than this?

It seems so unfair to change this pleasant group of children into an acne-riddled, size-obsessed collection of tantrums. Of course I exaggerate, Lord, but you know what I mean.

There are so many hazards that they face; so many chances to be scarred by events or words; so many opportunities to make a wrong decision, or to be the victim of someone else's wrong decision.

How do we help, Lord? Who can guide them through this maze? What can we teach? When can we offer support and friendship?

Lord, into your hands . . .

# About sex, drugs, rock and roll

Lord, a colleague suggested that I should talk to you about this topic. I don't know where to start. Our children and young people are under such subtle pressure, Lord, and it is so clever, so evil.

'Why not try . . . ?'

'What, are you scared or something?'

'Everyone's doing it; it's only a bit of fun.'

'No one will know; and anyway, who cares?'

'Just once won't make any difference.'

It's all lies, Lord! Every action makes a difference; every decision changes the world.

Why have 'wait' and 'no' become such neglected words?

Why can't there be pleasure in simple things; in things at the right time and in due season?

I know, Lord, I am an inhibited old reactionary who is sometimes just a bit jealous of the freedom and confidence of the young. But, Lord, in their freedom, in their confidence, keep them safe, if not in everything, at least from the big dangers.

# A reflection on bullying –
# An introduction

You will know about this, Lord, of course, but I want to talk about it anyway.

Bullying, Lord: the big, the strong, the quick-witted, picking on the weak, the slow and the dull.

Why does it happen?

We have school policies about it. We have staff meetings. We teach that it is wrong. We all know what we should do when it happens, but it is still a shock. It still takes us unawares.

However hard we try to prevent it, it still breaks out.

Why?

Original sin? Well, yes, of course; but why *this* sin?

Lying and theft are so much easier to understand – so much easier to deal with – so why bullying?

Can I stop here, Lord, and break it down a little? Talk to you about it bit by bit?

# A reflection on bullying – The bully

Sometimes bullies hit out: physically hurt their victims.

What makes them do this?

Usually we call them cowards; we challenge them to 'Pick on someone your own size.' Is it really fear and, if so, fear of what?

Sometimes bullies use power to threaten: do not attack, only threaten to do so. If they are powerful, why should they be fearful? What should they fear?

Lord, help us to help fearful bullies face their own fear, rather than exploit the fear of others.

And then there are the other bullies, Lord. Those whose words wound: who use speech like a surgical knife to cut out the confidence of their victim, sometimes deliberately, more often, apparently, without thought.

The gift of a quick wit is a responsibility; help us to help them use it wisely and well.

And here is the problem, Lord: we know what to do after the event; after the bullying; after the sin. We can sometimes prevent the occurrences by using our authority. But what are we doing to help the sinner?

Help us and guide us, Lord.

# A reflection on bullying –
# Those who look on

And all that talk of the sinner brings me to
another group.

What about those who know what is going on
and yet do nothing, or – worse – take pleasure
in watching from the sidelines?

What about them?

We get angry easily with such people; righteous
indignation abounds. But what about their fear;
their insecurity; perhaps their exploitation of others?

How do we develop their moral outrage, so that it
overcomes their fear, their security in the crowd,
their hesitant shyness?

What are we doing, Lord, about these folk? In
any incident they are probably in the majority.
What do we do about the bystander?

Help us and guide us, Lord.

# A reflection on bullying –
# The victim

And then there are the victims, whom we console
and support at the point of crisis.

To whom we sometimes seem to offer only
sticking plasters to mend their broken bones
and broken hearts.

What are we doing about the victims?

Is it true that some people are natural victims;
that they attract bullying as some people attract
compliments or lovers?

If so, we should be doing something about it, Lord.
How do we build them up, so that they no longer
present soft targets, easy meat for the vultures?

How do we make them secure and confident in
their difference, their uniqueness?

Help us and guide us, Lord.

# A reflection on bullying – Those in authority

And finally, there are those in authority.

Us, Lord.

Who are so often, bigger, stronger and quicker-witted than those over whom we have authority.

What do the bullies, the bystanders, the victims learn from us?

I don't mean when we are angry or offended that there has been an incident of bullying; I mean all the time.

Do we use fear – exploit our power over others – or do we show the bullies a better way to relate to others?

And while I am on this, Lord, 'fear' seems to come up constantly in these reflections. Is everyone afraid? Are everyone's actions governed by fear?

You sent your Son so we should have life abundantly, and yet we are shrivelled by our fears: physical fear; fear of failure; fear of change; sometimes even fear of success.

Lord, if fear is the key to all of this, help us to shed our fears and to live as you would have us live – abundantly.

Help us and guide us, Lord.

# Prayers around
the school year

# The empty classroom –
# Beginning of a new year

The room is shiny, clean and empty. There are no
pictures on the walls, no crisp packets behind the
radiators; the floors gleam with seal. The corridors
are quiet, save for the muted greetings of colleagues.

Someone once told me that schools were nice places
when the children were not in them. Quiet buildings
where you could work and think in plenty of space,
with the opportunity to make coffee and talk to
relaxed colleagues when you chose.

Well, Lord, in a sense it's true. They are calm and
stable, easy to move about in; but, rather like a
sailing-ship in a flat calm, they are going nowhere
and without real purpose.

So let me get on with it, Lord; let me prepare today,
for tomorrow the children arrive and this place will
not be calm and stable, easy to move about in. It will
be like a sailing-ship in a force six breeze; it will be
alive and about its business; and I shall be part of it.

# For Harvest

I could get quite enthusiastic about this, Lord.
What an opportunity Harvest offers to focus
all our teaching about interdependence, global
responsibility and eating the proper food. There
is a big project here, Lord: really solid teaching
about ideas that matter.

And yet, perhaps we drown it, Lord, in our concern
with bringing gifts to give to the poor. Of course
that is important too; but what are our pupils
learning here, while we sing endless verses of
'All things bright and beautiful' and Rosie drops
a bag of flour, which, being much handled, bursts
on the floor?

Who was exploited so that we could give our bags
of flour to the poor, Lord? Tough question, that;
difficult to think through.

And then again, which harvest are we celebrating?
There is very little harvesting in this area, except
from gardens and allotments, and that goes on for
quite a bit of the year. Many of the fields were cut
in August; some of the pupils will have seen this
on their way to and from holiday.

I am thinking my way into difficulties again, Lord.
What do you want us to celebrate during this
festival without a story?

We could do with some help, I think.

# Before a parents' evening

Dear Lord, tonight the parents are coming!

They want to hear about their children's progress.
They have hopes and dreams for their children,
on which they want me to pour encouragement.

I too have hopes and dreams for their children. Why
are they different from their parents' aspirations?

Lord, we have to communicate: to share our
experience of the children, so that together we
can help the children to make reality from their
own dreams, not ours.

The school frightens some parents; it brings back
memories of their own schooldays. Their fear shows
in timidity and in aggression; in silence and in things
half said. Help me to reassure and encourage them
and to listen patiently to the thoughts behind
their words.

And, Lord, I am sometimes frightened too: of the
aggressive parents; of those who should complain
because we have failed their children; and of those
who will complain even when we have succeeded.

Help me to control my fears, as I seek to calm the
fears of others.

Help me to be honest and fair in what I say, so that the results of this evening bear fruit for the children.

# For the autumn term

It is raining again; that makes four days this week, and it is only Thursday. Where is your mercy here, Lord? Have you any idea what a school feels like after a week of rain? Pupils and teachers trapped inside the building, with no relief from the gathering smell of wet coats and boots drying over hot radiators.

To ask if we are getting on each other's nerves is like asking if Muhammad Ali could box. And now the hall roof is leaking, and the lunch queue is being silly about it.

Dear Lord, a little intervention in the world weather patterns would be deeply appreciated. I would not mind frost; wind would at least dry things off a bit; just as long as it stops raining, Lord.

We enjoyed St Luke's little summer – the Headteacher did his usual assembly about it – but that was weeks ago. Now it is November and it is raining; without relief the pupils and I will grow in mutual intolerance by the hour.

Lord, in your mercy, give us the strength to endure; but better still, stop the rain!

# For All Souls' Day

It is getting dark, Lord. The days are drawing in,
but it is not just that the length of daylight is shorter.
Somehow, at this time of year the world seems a
darker place spiritually. Maybe this is encouraged
by the energy that some put into Hallowe'en and
all the negative images that it presents.

So I want to talk to you about something different.
Through All Saints' and All Souls' Days the Church
celebrates the lives of good Christians, and I want
to thank you for one of them.

In case you have not yet worked it out, Lord, it's Mrs
Johnston. You know her well. She cleans my part of
the school, and there is always one great smile on her
face when I arrive in the morning. I can't help smiling
back. That really helps get my day off to a good start,
even when the traffic has been terrible.

She talks about you so naturally and easily, knows
you as a friend and obviously has a great time
worshipping you at her church. She cleans there
as well as in school.

So, at this gloomy, dreary, oppressive time of year,
thank you for Mrs Johnston, Lord, whose smile lights
up the dark mornings.

# For Advent

It is the end of November. Two weeks and four days to go to the end of term, and counting. There is so much to do; so many things that must be finished before term ends. I do not know where the time goes. And soon it will be Christmas. Shopping, Lord, and the cards to do. It is so busy, Lord, so busy!

And they tell me that this is Advent: a time for reflection, penitence and preparation for the coming of your Son. The way we do it in this school, Lord, it is all about the commemoration of the first coming of your Son in Bethlehem; except, of course, for schools his was a premature birth, around a week or ten days early, which would have meant that he was born in Nazareth!

Sorry, Lord, being silly there; it is that time of term and that time in my life.

So where was I? Oh, yes, Advent: the preparation for the coming of your Son. If he came tomorrow, Lord, would we be ready? I can think of several colleagues who, as he descended in glory, with the last trump sounding, would react with 'Can you hang on a bit? I must get these reports done and I'm teaching 3L in ten minutes!' We would be quite unready and – the way things are this Advent – we won't be any more ready in the next three weeks.

Come, Lord Jesus; but preferably in the summer holidays, when we have the time.

# Before the school play

The school is in a state of high drama, Lord. Tonight the school play opens. Suddenly everything is intensely theatrical. There are tantrums, sulks, tearful reconciliations and panics about phantom illnesses amongst the leading members of the cast – and that is only in the staff room! Costumes are being frantically stitched together. The musicians are talking about dropping one of the songs, or at least changing the key. Those of us who only sell the tickets and count the takings remain coolly aloof from all this fevered activity. 'It will be fine', we say. 'It always is. Anyway, it's a sell-out, so why worry?' We get glared at. 'You don't understand', they say. But we do.

This is the point in the year, Lord – almost the only one – when the school comes together to support and use the creativity of staff and pupils working together. With the creativity come all those fantasies about 'what might have been' or 'what might yet be'. We discover hidden talents, or focus and use skills that are only just beginning to develop, in a glorious rush of creativity.

There will be forgotten lines, missed notes and falling scenery, certainly; but there will also be emerging talent, new triumphs and probably some laughter and applause.

So, Lord, for your blessing, the annual school play –
on with the motley – amen.

# For the Christmas holidays

And so it is Christmas. They gave me sixteen
handkerchiefs, three key rings, a wallet, a miniature
bottle of whisky and what feels like a dose of flu.
I gave them a Mars bar and a packet of felt pens
each and a term of my best teaching. A fair exchange,
Lord, to celebrate the birth of your Son?

Well, we did that too, of course: shepherded them all
through the rain to the local church and sang carols.
Then there was the nativity play to retell the story,
with metres of white sheeting and a flutter of angels.

Sorry, Lord, I am sounding cynical; it must be the flu,
or the whisky. It is just that somehow I think that we
missed it again: the point, that is. Your Son born in
Bethlehem at the start of the most important period
in the history of the world, and we celebrate it, not
in awe and thanksgiving, but with runny-nosed
shepherds and out-of-tune songs. But there again,
during the play I saw some of the parents in tears,
and when Harry sang the first verse of 'Away in a
manger' there was a lump in my throat; so perhaps . . .

And term is over and the festival and the flu are to
come. Lord of the universe, creator of the stars, thank
you for the traditional school Christmas and . . .

Bless me!

# At the beginning of the spring term

All through Christmas, Lord, I was too tired to really celebrate the coming of your Son; but then, you knew that. I was just getting into the swing of things, waking up, feeling human again, when here we are, back in school.

The spring term: Lord, what a silly name! Outside, the snow is falling into slush-filled streets, and the sparrows cough bronchitically as they cower in the gutters.

The pupils are reluctantly dragging themselves back through the weather. Some of them bring in shiny new presents that they hope to use in school; most, sensibly, leave such things at home, where they will be safer. And it occurs to me that today is the feast of the Epiphany: the day when we celebrate the coming of the wise men and the gifts that they brought to Jesus, foreshadowing his future, both good and bad.

What gifts are we giving to our pupils, Lord, to prepare them for their future? A general education, of course; but more specifically? The wise men brought three gifts to your Son. If we could give three gifts to our pupils, as a result of their time here, what would we want those gifts to be?

Food for thought there, Lord. I can feel a professional development day coming on – if only we weren't so tied up in literacy and numeracy.

# For Candlemas

Light is so important to us, Lord; it lifts our moods and raises our hopes. So today, as we hope winter is beginning to draw to an end, we celebrate your Son as the Light of the World.

I came into school in the dark this morning; I had some work to do before school started. Most of the classrooms were lit and you could see the building from quite a distance. A thought struck me: how does it shine in terms of spiritual things? I have heard some schools described as beacons of hope. Is ours like that, Lord? Should it be?

Last term, as the darkness gathered, we celebrated the individuals who keep the light of faith shining. At this point we celebrate the way in which your Son shines with a light that disperses the darkness and gathers the other lights to himself.

As we strive and struggle to educate our pupils, Lord, do we provide a light that gathers and focuses their hopes and dreams into a beacon that conquers the darkness?

A beacon of hope, Lord? It would be worth coming in early on a dark morning if that was what we could be.

# At the beginning of Lent

One of my colleagues has just announced that she is going to give up chocolate biscuits for Lent. Good for her! It will be difficult, but I am sure that she will rise to the challenge. It set me thinking though, Lord: funny time of year, Lent.

The second half of the term when we get all the work done. A period of solid effort, sandwiched between the Christmas celebrations and the exams and sports days of the summer term. What do we do for Lent?

Spiritual discipline? Well, yes; we are into spiritual development in this school.

Penitence? Yes again; we are always trying to make pupils feel sorry for their misdeeds.

Reflection? That is what school worship is for, isn't it?

So what are we doing about Lent? Well, there is the ban on chocolate biscuits in the staff room, but doing something extra – no time, Lord, no time! Perhaps we *could* just find five minutes each day to stop and think: to admire the primroses, or to give thanks for a little victory in the classroom, or a breakthrough in the school budget negotiations.

Just five minutes to pause in the day? Worth a try, Lord; it has to be better than going without chocolate biscuits for six whole weeks.

# For Easter time

It's a holiday again, Lord, and some of my colleagues are off attending conferences. Where do they get their energy?

Most of us are using the break to catch our breath and to worry about all the things that our pupils should have learned by now and all the things that they are forgetting during the holiday period.

And then there is Easter: the great drama of the death and resurrection of your Son, which we so easily domesticate with buns, chocolate eggs and spring flowers.

And yet, the promise of new life, Lord . . . It seems to me that because we are so used to an annual cycle of renewal we forget the power of this promise.

In our own small way, there is the offer of new life through education: the chance to break out of the 'like father, like son' tradition; to grasp the opportunities for which the abilities that you have given have equipped us. We should reflect on the labourer's daughter who becomes a doctor, with all the dramatic changes that represents in a single generation.

The new life you offer is more dramatic, more fundamental, than that. At this Easter time, Lord, help us to grasp a little more of its true significance.

# Before the school fête

Here it comes again, Lord: the annual event known
by the cynics in the staff room as 'the fate worse
than death'. Yes, I am referring to the annual Parent
Teacher Association fête on the school playing-field.

Yes, I do know that it is important, I know that it
raises a great deal of money for the school and it is
also a useful social occasion, but ... Well, to tell the
truth, I am hiding, Lord. The deputy head is looking
for volunteers to have wet sponges thrown at them
by the top year. It is not my turn – I did it last year –
so I am in hiding until her rota is full. Last year was a
disaster. I forgot to bring a change of clothes and had
to wander around the fête, soaked to the skin, being
polite to parents. It was just my luck to meet the
chair of governors *after* my turn as a sponge target,
rather than before. Your sense of humour there, Lord?

I try to maintain an image of serious professionalism
when I am in the company of school governors. When
the chair saw me at last year's fête, however, she
just laughed.

So on Saturday, Lord, let it be fine. The fête really
must be a success. No wet sponges, please Lord,
and not too many ice-cream-smothered baby
brothers and sisters to meet and smile at while they
wipe their sticky hands on whatever they can reach.

# Before pupils do a test or examination

I don't suppose that you have time for this, Lord, but I am nervous. Not for myself, but for my class. Today they have that test, Lord; the one that seems to determine their future.

They have worked hard; so have I!

They deserve to do well.

It should not be a problem, but . . . well, you know this lot, Lord.

They can get so silly if they are nervous or excited.

They forget things that normally they know, like their names and the date! O Lord, they are in there, and there is nothing I can do but worry.

Keep them calm, Lord.

Keep them focused.

Let them do their best.

At this moment they really need your help.

# For Ascension Day

I have this picture of your Son's ascension, Lord;
heavily influenced by medieval artists, no doubt.
I see him rising into the clouds, while down
below his disciples look mystified, frightened and
uncertain, worried about what will happen next.

Was this how it happened?

Probably not, but never mind. It occurs to me that
we have an experience with some elements of
that, but in reverse. From now until the end of the
summer term some of our pupils will be leaving us.

They go up to a bigger school; or to a university;
or into the big wide world. They look mystified,
frightened and uncertain, worried about what will
happen next.

We, who are left behind, have to let them go –
difficult that, sometimes. We worry about what
will happen to them: have we taught them enough,
equipped them properly for the future? We wonder
how they will survive in an alien environment and
how far they will stay true to what we have tried
to teach them.

Did your Son feel like that? No, of course not; you are all-seeing and all-knowing. That must make for confidence.

For us ordinary humans, however, letting go can be hard, Lord.

# A thanksgiving

I don't believe it!

They did it!

It was a struggle, but they tried so hard and they did it!

Thank you, Lord, for this moment; for their success; for my relief.

When things are tough next year, let me remember this feeling!

Let me remember how proud I feel of this group, and how hard it seemed for them when we started.

Let me remember that this group did it, and if they can, anyone can. Not just the talented few, the ones that we rely on, but all of them. O Lord, the smiles on some of their faces! I can see the confidence growing, the self-doubt falling away. They stand taller, walk straighter.

It is great!

Lord, thank you again, for they did it; and maybe, just maybe, I helped a bit.

# A prayer of anger

How are you with thunderbolts these days, Lord?
Have you got a good supply? Is your aim still good?
I ask because they are at it again: the knockers, the
'we had it harder in our day' brigade, claiming that,
if the results are good, the exams are too easy –
yet again.

I saw those youngsters through two years of struggle
and effort. I saw them bouncing with delight when
they read their results. Now I have watched the
bouncing fade, as the idiots pour scorn on their
achievements.

So bring down the thunderbolts!

Teach them to praise; failing that, if they are
really slow learners, teach them to be quiet!

Not Christian? We should turn the other cheek?
Yes, I know, but did you see the looks on those
young people's faces?

I know! I know! I must forgive; but couldn't you
manage one little one? A near miss would do:
a thunderbolt that passes over the interviewer's
shoulder and lands between the pundit's toes.
Just a little one? Please?

I know all that is wrong. I must forgive. It is probably better to keep silent, because tomorrow the media will have forgotten all this and the young people will have their certificates for ever, but thank you for listening, anyway.

# The empty classroom – End of a school year

Well, Lord, they have gone. The echoes of their words, their shouts, their tears, are dying down the corridors. The crisp packets are settling with the dust and the school falls silent. As I gaze around the room I am sad, happy and tired. Lord, I am tired.

I am sad to see them go: the ones I enjoyed teaching, the ones who challenged and argued, those who thought and those who responded. I shall miss them. When I see them around the school next year, even when I teach them, they will not be the same. They will have moved on and I shall have a new group. Yes, I shall miss the pupils they were yesterday.

I am happy to see them go: the ones who were a battle, the ones who were a challenge, those who did not seem to learn much and those who learned without me. I shall not miss them; next year they will have moved on and so shall I.

I am tired to my bones, Lord. I ran out of energy weeks ago. Next year, I swear, I will pace myself better, so that I arrive at this point with something in hand for the holidays; for friends and family; for myself. I think I promised that last year as well, but . . . this year I mean it.

And so the room is quiet and they are gone, my desk is clear and I must go too; go home to bed, to sleep, to dream, perchance not to wake up until the day after tomorrow.

# Prayers for colleagues and ourselves

# A prayer of an overworked headteacher

It was a quiet day. Thank you. Work got done; not all that I hoped to do, but, well, I must count my blessings.

I dealt with all the interruptions to the interruptions. For that mercy, thank you, Lord.

I dealt with most of the interruptions, but I think that I forgot one or two. May they not turn into tomorrow's disasters! For that mercy, thank you, Lord.

I did *some* of the work I planned to do today; I even completed some tasks. For that minor miracle, thank you, Lord.

And, yes, now I remember it, I taught a lesson uninterrupted and even smiled at a pupil or two. I remember their puzzled faces!

It was truly a good, solid day.

Thank you, Lord, and in my thanks a small request: dear Lord, could it possibly be the same again tomorrow?

# For a colleague about to retire

He has gone about his work in the school quietly, solidly, for years. Generations of pupils have learned maths through his teaching, and some have learned to love the subject; no mean feat, Lord! Last week he had two letters at school. One was from a former pupil, letting him know that she had got a first and was going on to do a master's degree. The other was from an angry parent, complaining that her daughter was being forced to learn about square roots, 'whatever they are', instead of something useful. The teacher's lot does not change!

Now – today – I learned that he is to retire at the end of the term. It is strange to think of the place without him.

There will be a party, naturally, and the usual words will be said. How do you sum up the work of someone who has given a lifetime to solid teaching: nurturing talent where it could be found; developing basic knowledge in those with no special gifts; and patiently working away with the strugglers?

Good work, honest work, valuable work, now coming to an honourable end.

How do we say this, Lord? How can we make sure that he knows the value of his work, the respect of his colleagues, as he moves into retirement? What we say in these last few weeks may need to last him twenty years. May we say the right words, and may he hear the love behind them.

# For a colleague experiencing difficulties

I want to talk to you about Jonesy. You know about his problems, Lord. You know the way he feels as he comes to school. He seems to drag himself in from the car park in the morning. He drags himself to his room and the pupils sense his weaknesses, his lack of energy. By the end of the day he seems to be drawn, hunched, beaten; then tomorrow it starts again.

It wasn't always like this, Lord; last year he did well enough, and for his first three years we all thought he had the makings of a really good colleague.

What has happened?

We can't get close to him.

Nothing seems to help; neither the support of colleagues nor the targets and training given him by senior colleagues seem to touch him.

We are at our wits' end, Lord. What do we do? We do what we can, but we know that without you it will not be enough, so I bring him to you, Lord. We offer our colleague up to your love and care.

# For a brilliant teacher

I had to watch her teach today, Lord, as part of the appraisal process. At the end of the lesson she asked me what I thought, and when I didn't answer at once her face began to fall.

'Give it to me straight,' she said. 'I trust your judgement. Was it all right?'

Still I hesitated. She blundered on.

'I wasn't sure about that story; should I have read it rather than told it? What do you think?'

At last I found my voice. I told her it had been a privilege to be in the lesson; that I thought it was wonderful and that she was a gifted storyteller. Her mouth fell open.

'You're kidding! It's just what everyone does – nothing special. I tell stories like that all the time.'

I mumbled like a schoolboy on a first date. She must have thought me mad. I left her room determined to do better myself, to work at what I do well and to learn from her.

What a gift you have given her, Lord! What an experience for those pupils in her classes! What a gift for this school while she is here!

What a pair of fools we must have looked: the one unable to give praise properly and clearly to a colleague and the other unable to accept it.

Thank you, Lord, that, despite the pressure to be dull, there are still brilliant teachers and our school has one.

# For a new teacher

I met her this morning, Lord. She was smiling bravely, but obviously very nervous. Who would not be, coming in to meet new colleagues in her first teaching post? It is so hard starting your teaching career; it was easy to see that she was feeling the strain.

Be with her, Lord; give her confidence, or at least enable her to act as if she was confident.

Now she is sitting in her room, looking at the desks. Are you with her, Lord? Of course you are; silly question; sorry! Is that a quiet moment's thought or the paralysis of panic? The former: she is up and moving about, changing things round, setting it up the way that she wants it. May these early decisions be good ones.

Everything should be fine; she has a good degree and the reports from her training are excellent. But this is different. This is the real world of professional accountability, and there is no one to take responsibility on her behalf. Be with her tomorrow, Lord, when the pupils arrive. Protect her from too many early mistakes. Give her a good start, so that she can become the teacher that you want her to be.

# For a headteacher

As she went into the Head's room, Lord, I offered Jade up to you. You remember: the Head called her 'the worst-behaved girl in the school'.

It has struck me, Lord, thinking about it, that I should have offered up the Headteacher to you as well.

Sorry, Lord; another sin of omission – they get me every time!

What a job, Lord! In the middle of balancing next year's budget, the Head learned this morning that the Deputy has got promotion and is leaving next term. Then, to crown it all, I sent in Jade for the third time this week. No wonder she used her 'playground voice', Lord. It must be so frustrating.

And there is no one to turn to – no one to share it with – and the issues must be dealt with, because the buck stops in that room.

I am sorry that I left her out of the prayer for Jade.

So, as I go to talk to her now to discuss what can be done about Jade, Lord, remember the Head and sustain her. Give her the gift of patience – with governors, administrators, naughty children and, perhaps, also with me.

# Before an inspection

The inspection is this week. Help! My knees feel weak,
my stomach cramps up and my brain turns to mush.
I have been snapping at friends, family and my pupils.
What is wrong with me?

I am a professional.

I prepare my work carefully.

My pupils are learning; I can demonstrate their
progress.

Why, Lord, do I feel like a student on his first
teaching practice?

My colleagues and my pupils need me to be calm,
confident and in control. I can do it, Lord; I can do
it, but only with your help.

So it is inspection this week and I need your help.

Help me, Lord, lest I drown.

# Before leading an act of school worship

Lord, I know that many of those gathered here
know little of you, or of how you should be
worshipped and loved. In what I say and do, may
they learn more about how you might be honoured
in their thoughts, in their prayers and in their lives.

# Before an important day in school

Lord, this is a key day for us.

We need your help, and during the day we may
get so tied up in what we are doing that we
forget to ask again.

So be with us, Lord, to help, support and guide.
You are all-seeing and all-knowing. Today, Lord,
be the eyes in the backs of our heads.

# Before marking

I have three piles of books to mark, Lord,
all of them due back tomorrow.

As I plough through the work, mindful of the
school's policy on marking, let me avoid blame, Lord.
It is not necessarily their fault that they have not
understood my lesson, nor is it necessarily mine.
Maybe it was just a bad day for attention. It was
snowing, as I recall. I cannot be a super-teacher
every day. To be honest, being a super-teacher just
occasionally would be good.

Let me look for the positive: identify signs of hope
and respond to those, so that we all move on.

Why I am so negative about this, Lord? I am
assuming that they will have made a mess of it.
Why do I do that? Perhaps they will have
understood. Perhaps I will have taught it well.

Lord of all hopefulness, let me mark hopefully. Let
me remember that it was *not* you who said, 'Blessed
are those who expect nothing, for they shall never
be disappointed.'

You saw the potential for good in all, so let me
be optimistic, Lord. There are, after all, only ninety
books to mark by breakfast time.

# Reflection on a staff room

Well, Lord, here we are in the one pupil-free place in the school, apart from the boiler room and the kitchen. This should be a safe place for adults, Lord: one place where we can relax, prepare our work, mark, meet colleagues, think and plan. It should be a place of recreation and mutual support. So why do we squabble about who has used whose coffee mug, or who is sitting in whose chair? Why do we avoid 'unsafe' topics of discussion, and who decided they were unsafe? And why is the place so untidy? If it were up to me, of course, things would be better. It's just that some of my colleagues are so . . .

Sorry, Lord. I was just getting into a good moan when I remembered that part of your Son's teaching about the speck of dust in your brother's eye and the beam of timber in your own.

So what am I going to do to make the staff room a better place for my colleagues? How am I going to support them and respect their concerns and their lives? I feel that there is a challenge here. You are good at those, aren't you, Lord? Well, with your help I will try – but does it mean all of them, Lord?

Sorry; silly question.

I'm good at those, aren't I?

# Paths to praying

# Developing a cycle of prayer: some ideas

Busy teachers often say that it is difficult to make time to pray. The round of preparation, marking and working on the latest new initiative can quickly eat into the time available outside the classroom. For many it does not seem to leave enough time for family, friends and interests outside school, let alone time to talk to God.

The ideas in the next few pages do not assume that there will be much time available each day, but do provide a way of creating a sharp focus for the time of prayer, however short that has to be.

# Ways of praying

Ideally, everyone should make time for prayer,
but making space every day can be difficult.
Here are two ways of praying that may help
you to make good use of the time that you have.

## The quickest way

If you are really pushed for time, simply focus
on the subject of your prayer and hold it up to
God. Don't try to form words; just picture yourself
holding the individual or group up for God's
loving care and attention.

## A more reflective way

If you have a few minutes to spare, think about
the individual pupils, classes or people. What do you
like about them? What do they find difficult? What
bores them? What excites them? What is happening
at the moment in their lives at home, in school or
elsewhere? Then form a prayer, based on these
thoughts, which focuses on their needs and the
effectiveness of your work with them. In the section
on prayers for children you may find some which help
you to do this; occasionally one of them might be
directly appropriate for one of your classes.

## Primary teachers – Praying the register, a monthly cycle

Most primary teachers have responsibility for a class of children, usually, but not always, between twenty-five and thirty. If each day you focus a short prayer on a single name on your register, taking each child's name in turn, you will have prayed for every child in the class specifically at least once a month.

## Secondary teachers – Praying the timetable

Teachers in secondary schools see so many pupils in the course of a week that it would be very difficult to set up a system that enabled regular prayer for individual pupils. Given the pressure on time, it is probably more useful to pray for each class that you teach on a weekly basis. A simple grid for the week, like the one illustrated here, could be used for this purpose. You may decide to put each class in on the first day that you teach them in the week; or the day after you have taught them; or on the day when they are doing homework based on your lessons. It is up to you, but each class should appear on the grid once a week. You may want to remember to create a space each week for those classes that you will have to cover for colleagues. Possibly Sunday, when you may have more time, is the best day of the week to focus on your own tutor group.

| Class or group | | |
|---|---|---|
| Sunday | | |
| Monday | | |
| Tuesday | | |
| Wednesday | | |
| Thursday | | |
| Friday | | |
| Saturday | | |

# Headteachers: Two approaches

## (i) Praying the school structure

Headteachers and others with management responsibilities in the school may approach the structure of their prayers rather differently from teachers whose main responsibility is in the classroom. Using the grid shown, they should focus first on a year group for each day of the week. In primary schools with nursery classes, Sunday could be used for the Foundation stage; it is probably the day when there is more time available for prayer, so greater time can be given to reflecting in your prayers the specific needs of this stage. Alongside a particular year group there will need to be prayers for the adults involved with the school. These

|           | Year group | Staff & governors |
|-----------|------------|-------------------|
| Sunday    |            |                   |
| Monday    |            |                   |
| Tuesday   |            |                   |
| Wednesday |            |                   |
| Thursday  |            |                   |
| Friday    |            |                   |
| Saturday  |            |                   |

should be split up so that every adult working
in the school is covered at least once each week.

One possible way would be to pray for the teachers
involved with each key stage in the school on a
different day (three days maximum); the staff who
administer the school or care for the building and
its surrounds, the staff who prepare meals or
supervise the pupils; volunteers; and the governing
body. Which day you use for which is up to you,
but some factors may influence your choices. For
example, if your governors routinely use a particular
day of the week for their meetings, it would make
sense to pray for them on that day.

(ii) Praying the keys

A different way for headteachers to structure
their prayers for the school is to use their sets
of keys. This works particularly well where there
are separate keys for different parts of the school.
As you hold each key separately, pray for that part
of the school; staff and pupils who work in it;
and those who will visit that part of the school
during the day.